Retirement Clock

Jim Bennett

Poems 5

Retirement Clock

Poetry is about truth, yet this is a work of fiction in that names of places and characters are used purely for convenience. Any resemblance to actual persons, living or dead, events, or locales, is entirely coincidental.

All rights reserved.
Copyright © 2014 Jim Bennett
www.jim-bennett.ca

No part of this work may be reproduced in any form or by any means, electronic and mechanical, including photocopying, recording, or by any retrieval system without prior written permission from the copyright holder.

Cover Image and Design by Rory d'Eon
Visit deon.ca to find Rory and his products and services!
Original (atrocious) cover photograph by Jim Bennett
(Clock presented by IBM Canada Limited)

Published by Lulu.com

ISBN 978-0-9881258-8-9

Acknowledgements

I owe a debt of gratitude to everyone who ever criticized or encouraged me. I am especially grateful to the writers group which critiques me so effectively that I can hardly ever leave anything dumb or unfinished in a poem. Thank you for refocussing my blind eye.

I would also like to thank those upon whom I have visited my opinion as a Kindle Book Review team member; many of you have been helpful and returned my efforts with insights and promotional assistance. I would like to specifically mention here Inge H. Borg (several books), who has featured me on her websites; Jon P Gunn, who as 'one who was there,' commented on Polaris (Jon is the author of The Apes of Eden), and Robert Nicholas (Shaker Lane), who mentioned me kindly on his book cover. I apologize to others not mentioned here due to lack of space or my poor memory.

I would like to thank Chelsea Rainford for trusting me with an informal review of an intensely personal work, a book of poetry; and Gisela Sherman for allowing me to comment on her entire marvellous novel of the farmerettes during World War I. These forthcoming books will each be a sensation. Different and powerful.

I owe a lifelong debt to Richard Ketchum, who taught me that "the statute of limitations is crap," that I can do this.

For this book in particular I would like to acknowledge the effort and insights of Sandra Aitken and Deborah Serravalle, who checked and commented on the entire volume. Thank you.

I again thank Rory d'Eon for a neat cover image. Rory creates marvels from my clumsy snapshots.

I won't thank IBM for the clock, particularly; but it did inspire the title poem of this volume.

Finally I must thank my wife Patricia, whose support and encouragement have always been there, in tough moments as well as in the good times. We've travelled together in more senses than one. It must be weird to have someone suddenly pull out a notebook and scribble nonsense - anywhere, any place, any time. Fortunately one of us is a practical person. She sits down while creating.

Table of Contents

View, Finder	1
Too Late	2
Pictures of Children (for my children)	4
for Gary Lautens	6
My Fellow Passengers	7
Two Senior Citizens in Six Cinquains	8
ToothPick, NoteBook	10
Seconds	11
Camp Site	12
The Path Now Taken	14
Burning	16
Executed	17
Speech to the Statue of Liberty	18
From a Complex Dream	19
Polaris	20
Photographic Memory	22
Confetti	23
The Cry of the Frog (for Madeleine Albright)	24

Table of Contents

DebtLand	25
Peter Revson	26
Dinner with Niki	27
Images: Gilles Villeneuve	28
NoteBook: Galapagos' Worlds	30
Hiroshima	32
Cinquain 87: Matti's Flowers	33
From G Ross Lord Park	34
Afterward: in the Cemetery above the Reservoir	35
The Message of Gary Gilmore	36
The Silence of Gary Gilmore	37
Dream Meredith	38
Whipper Billy Watson	40
Evensong: What Time Has Left	42
Helmeted	43
A Work for Peanuts (for Charles Schultz)	44
The Satan Clause	45
Earl Goes to Egypt	46

Table of Contents

From Bexhill Court	47
What Happened to Campus Women?	48
Retirement Clock	49
Not Resolved	50
For the Next Night Train	52
Pirouette with a Rose in your Teeth	54
In Halifax Citadel	55
To Crows Returning	56
Old Tracks	57
Relapse	58
Drab Ending	59
In Thorn Wood	60
Baracoa: Max's World	62
Certificate for Tania	67
This is It	68
Goodbye	70
Moon Dreamer	71
The Lost Camp	72

View, Finder

Composed
the lake waits, tensioned
by a clouding sunset;
even small disturbances of minnows
or water beetles
snap frozen in its purple mirroring
where inverted shivering trees begin to bend
   across the water
a single leaf swoops into perfect focus
orange against the buckshot scattered sky
of the coming storm

If I turn this picture over
and whisper your name
will I see your old hand writing blurred notations
   some colour film what fraction of a second
for me the dead leaf always hovers
alive in my mind
trembling along my fingers feel the eyes
that hold the wires that fix the frame
if I turn this picture over

and the coming storm
finds me exposed as usual
composed

Jim Bennett   Poems 5

Too Late

Restless inside against the dark
and dozing on the last bus home
whose whining wheels raise rhythmic sentences:

Cornwall Brockville Gananoque
A-AS AS-BO BO-CA CA-CO
July twenty-one nineteen twenty-two
go back to sleep

Kingston Belleville Cobourg
CO-ED ED-FO FO-GY H-IT
May fifteen nineteen forty-one
relax relax relax

Oshawa Whitby Toronto
IT-LY M-NA NA-PE PE-PY
November 10 nineteen seventy-seven
stretch   out

Retirement Clock

Streetsville Cambridge Woodstock
Q-SC SC-ST ST-UN UN-ZY
last week: too late

Now it's all been said
to the dark by the grey coach rumbling home
swaying like dismal shadows come
too late too late remember

why towns passed in order
like dates in time
or old mnemonic guide words
reminding of the content, the knowledge lost
of your birth
           marriage
                      heart attack
                                death

as if the tires heard you whispering
come home: too late

Pictures of Children (for my children)

The really embarrassing part of cleaning house
is my own closet shelf
clutter is hardly the word for it
dust
on the ribbons of neglected diplomas
admittam te ad gradam
grey faces conjured
on a forgotten ledge of time
and beyond even these
are my high school journals
in the graduation newsletter
are awards and names let's look for the photo section
in the *Alderama*
for the dedications what nonsense we wrote
of strategies for losing the attendance register
let's go out to shoot pool
little black books and algebra homework
stop signs uniforms the crazy things kids mention
as the important stuff to be left behind
in the collective unconscious of memory
so seldom recalled

Retirement Clock

So I stand bemused in the closet doorway
with a shirtsleeve over one shoulder and fan the pages
looking
through this foolish wisdom for my own lost words
these were my friends
we made each others' worlds
for fun or not
               ate together
competed for marks and girls' approval
learned chess and football and beat each other

Even though not seen since these are not strangers
their voices echo and mingle with my own
in memory as immediate as my present speech
"you've got to have a look at this" and turning
to the photographs

They all look rather childish and even my own sure face
appears uncertain
as if it looked out but could not see this far
or perceive a universe of choices
to unfold discard exploit defend oneself from

as unbelievable as it must seem to you
I am still this person trapped in the page of time
this is was the me I am who feels
the same old passions

nevertheless
what time has taught could not have been explained
beforehand
to any of these waiting lives.

for Gary Lautens

Your truth
rejoiced all truth
your joy
        embraced a gift
for joy
        your love
                your truth could share
with love

My Fellow Passengers

III

watch this:
slim legs, tight jeans
thigh snug hip dimensions
strain visible, curves all the bus
must see

II

pink hair,
what does it say?
steel brow ring, what's it mean?

Tall attitude, far too hung up
to smile

I

   blunt face
blue-black eyes shift
 rude stare noticing now
the subway door reflecting back
   myself

Two Senior Citizens in Six Cinquains

Front porch
watching Kitty
grown up fifteen years, stretch
as stiffly as herself, just two
old girls

our days
wound up too fast
after moving children
slowed down at last, arthritic on
bad knees

one size
fits all the world
other things grew or shrank
but not the lap, the cat, herself
one size

Retirement Clock

eyes dimmed
by golden light
half-awake near sunset
dream catlike youth sleek supple limbs
dozing

till dusk,
stirring when rain
spatters front porch her face
wakes up disgusted as her cat
wants in

front porch
our days one size
eyes dimmed till dusk wants in
grown up slowed down fits all the world
old girls

ToothPick, NoteBook

Falling out of my notebook
my broken toothpick landed bent
into five odd-angled segments
on the mylar kitchen table it stopped
like a pale tall stalking heron
beak down, neck slanted, body, wading legs
bent poised
as if to stab into the waiting surface
and capture something it saw that I could not.
I was writing up my notes from Costa Rica
and you were gathering up the midnight snack.
We'll unpack in the morning
and take the films in Monday and pay the bills.
That's what it's like coming back here from vacation,
so quickly surrounded by our home reminders.
I'm glad we have photos notebooks and conversations
 - you must do a sketch from the one on the yellow beach -
and our trivial recollections:
did you see how the heron stood at the edge of water
waiting standing watching a world invisible
we can only enter now in imagination
with the aid of toothpicks images
and notes

Retirement Clock

Seconds

at the slope of jumbled stones you clambered ahead of me
it made you look taller
and for a few seconds I was four and a half again

when the chipmunk scattered fallen leaves underfoot
I was not startled as she was;
I had climbed past here before
setting up peanut shells as bait
wanting them less afraid of me, used to my smell
and my squeaking sneakers
hoping to hold one, talk to it for ten seconds,
I had stayed out far above the tiny cabin
the best part of two hours
until she called me down for suppertime
and would not let me come out again
- *he pretends far too much and spends too much time alone* -

- that was my mother speaking -
stop a minute and let me catch my bearings,
for an instant I forgot where we were
who you are
climbing back to the road by a talus of staggered boulders
when the chipmunk scattered my shadow made me feel shorter
I was four and a half years old

struggling up rocks large enough to be citadels castles
making up lures while moving softly on sneakers
for resident chipmunks scattering leaves like memories
searching for something hidden
or once imagined
and lost in my secret places

Camp Site

what is it about the orange tents
that are not here
on the field of grass and daisies
and why does the brook trill and trickle
pouring around the jar of powdered milk
that is not trapped in the tiny waterfall
what is the message beneath the breathless trees
that are not whispering secrets over
the sigh of wind on a nylon flap
nor hiding
the hiss of a pumped gas stove
ticking now as it stops shut off to cool
and the sunset dims to a dusky memory
of twilight haunted with owls and fireflies
calling to tell us fairy stories
for the city children
who wonder out loud why we have come to camp
from so long ago

Retirement Clock

not a footprint tent peg mark remains
no sign of the hole-dug latrine
or the pale cord clothesline rub on the maple bark
not a trace of the place where the tents or sleeping bags
bent back the grass
which tangles now around our turning feet
keeping us still reluctant to retreat
from the birdsong dawns and remember how loud at night
the creek became with everything dark awake
in the different silence: no traffic noise no sixty cycle hum
nothing but swaying trees
in the wild calm time still innocent
of any whispered thought for a careful future
safe in a couple of orange nylon tents
standing jauntily against their poles and peg cords
in that simple moonlit space
just where did we lie and what did we dream
that calls us back to wonder
on the field of grass and daisies

The Path Now Taken

your pathway into heaven
is not a path all choose to take
the path you leave on earth is not
a path you simply chose

facing life is like facing winter
in a strange cold climate without friends
or family to call or call on
waiting in a land of infidels
is infinite loneliness
without a common word of meaning

    on the television British actors pretend
    to enjoy their pubs and darts and draughts
    telling lies and lewd jokes that let out
    the poisons of their clerkly working lives

    but Americans have one life to live
    an all-sensuous drama of rich and sexual
    innuendo with no word for the kind of day
    that you have with beliefs that are secret, alien

        in a life that follows no laugh track
        and no suspenseful music plots your movements

Retirement Clock

so buy the tickets
arrange identity artifacts with cash
reread last briefing's letter
shower and dress
tighten clothes make sure the knife and call a cab
a tense few moments airport workers watch you
eyes darting suspiciously
X-ray your bag is that your carry-on
Let me Help you Find your Seat reLax
first class a final treat
at last the airframe shivers at push-back
now engines strain for takeoff wait for the time
and take your position quietly
remember how to hold the blade and butcher
first others then yourself and thousands

    the path you took
    demands the path ahead
    the path now chosen
    absolves your path behind

Burning

I am the flame of Vengeance come
this plane its blade beneath my thumb
to slash one tower banked with lies
and spill such sinners down dark skies
like blood of stewardess struck dumb

Crew, passengers, rich, weak, succumb;
let one phone home. the rest sit numb.
none see: beneath my shaved disguise
I am the flame.

God's airplane leans; their building, plumb;
white window faces see me from
a hundred yards: this heathen prize
transforms: a plume of burning eyes
praise Allah! thine I have become:
I am the flame

Executed

throat cut
blood slick cabin floor
struggle for cockpit door
can't shut

diving turn
banked wings slice three floors
explosive roars
we burn

shout
go down stairs
passage blocked by beams walls chairs
can't get out

phones calling
warble warning doomed sky scrapers
concrete desktops bodies papers
falling

scatter
bystanders cut to pieces
Dad's photograph my cousin nieces
rubble rain drops spatter

our dead
wait silently whose God explains
these executed plans remains
unsaid

Speech to the Statue of Liberty

I saw the flame of freedom fail
twin struck sky scrapers twist and wail
keen terror twice one hundred floors
collapsing: windows walls steel doors
crushed rubble panicked crowds inhale

held breathless by the grim travail,
pale rescuers hope turning frail,
faint flickered light from far dark shores:
I saw the flame

bid us rebuild. We dare not quail
for terrorists. Attack their trail:
make them regret such coward wars
on innocents. While your arm soars
this lamp of freedom must prevail.
I saw the flame.

From a Complex Dream

The complex dream that lured me back to sleep
dissolved in alarm bells seven minutes later
impossible to try to snooze again
so get up and find my clothes and shave for work
time to go, time to go
maybe a Druxy's coffee and cheddar bagel
if the traffic gets me downtown soon enough
rush hour honking orange lights
the occasional madman cell phone juggler weaving
could be late for a meeting am I prepared for mine
yes the notes and charts are fine with a power point diskette
and four colour handouts
under a cover page collage that glows like a travel brochure
vacation destination eye candy bikini distractions
there could be a promotion hidden in this
proposal
more likely another long dry talking session
in the cool board room that looks out over the islands
where somebody's tacking taking the wind to starboard
gulls wheeling
are there any final questions gentlemen
No the complex dream that lured me back to sleep
dissolved in alarm bells seven minutes later
a sabbatical has its advantages
it was time to get up and have a leisurely breakfast
then a walk by the creek and maybe a trip to the library
get a book about sailing another on shorebirds
check the back garden pick fresh vegetables
after I read the morning paper
including sections not marked Business Headlines
scanning Anne Landers laughing at horoscopes
"a day for project planning think out loud"
reminds me
of some weird and wild idea I had while waking
from a complex dream

Polaris

Grey dusk:
pale colour-changing dials betray
a beam-pierced outside ocean's darkening;
here under artificial night and day
messages come in: messages in two persons
because the persons sending messages
anticipate reply from this or that person
mute in the steel hull submerged.

Far forward in our submarine
whispers the genie of this world:
twenty-seven interconnected computers.
There is the screen which is his eye, and here
you can catch the straining of his ear.

One either side of the passageway, two huge
murmuring cylinders are his strength to move;
his strength to strike is farther back:
power in sixteen upright tubes
held at attention in rigid rows,
stiff trunks of a metal army, weapons waiting.

Farther aft still are quarters for men
who have no room to move.

Turbines throb and missiles wait
while men sleep, joke, and talk about the world
of messages come in:
all in unreal light where time is lost
and home drifts far away.

Retirement Clock

A man nudges a stick, the ship tilts up
as two great winglike rudders tilt
(and the missiles and computers tilt)
until the man relents, at weapons depth,
and signals, position for drill.

Men move, muscles and electrons move,
but our missiles wait - still missiles wait for targets,
roaming the world in an enchanted dungeon
to protect forgotten things: wild sunshine,
sheer open air, pure freedom to move:
these missiles protect, in their waiting tenseness.

The sub tilts down, and the men tilt,
and reread messages anticipating replies
because they may stay down for sixty days:
one hundred and twenty-four men, twelve officers,
two throbbing turbines, an eye and an ear
with twenty-seven computers
for sixteen silent sentries guarding at sea.

Photographic Memory

albums
just hold pictures
flat images forget
hello   the first smile   finding love
touching

Confetti

the storm of confetti is over: the ritual ended at sunset

this man you blushed beside in white veiled wonder
    accept his ring
    whom god hath joined let no man put asunder
the organ groaned
you clung to one tuxedo perfect arm
past aisle faces marching
blind flashbulbs crunched along the sidewalk

reception dinner
blur tinkled kissing glasses
white tiers of icing
your mother brooding in a shadow corner
dark eyes caressing
rough laughter are you leaving early
or coming late
the party roars behind you
black borrowed car crepe paper ribbons flutter
horns chime in twilight

confetti shower falls your hair undoing
unveil before the watchful mirror
tuxedo shoulders crumple on the doorknob
whose flesh arms grope around you
reflections echo deepest organ groaning
accept this ring
with pink silk sliding downward
fresh printed sheets lie open waiting
whom god hath joined shy awkwardness
caressing
as drunken relatives in partying
forget themselves
the storm of confetti is over

The Cry of the Frog
(for Madeleine Albright)

It was my mistake
something big moved and surprised me
when I jumped at once this snake was on me
fangs piercing lungs in spikes of pain
It's hard to die quiet crushed in darkness
swallowed up by a savage chewing

It was no mistake
I saw the snake and sent it the other way
so when the frog jumped up in front of my shoe
the snake was right on it
moved so fast
I could hear the cry of the frog

It was someone's mistake
something huge came and shook us awake in the night
explosions roared everywhere
while flames diving down from the sky
lit building walls torn apart in sections of concrete
then twisted iron beams inside them broke out
like bones of shrieking torture victims
we found ourselves crushed, falling in darkness
lungs bursting

It was no mistake
our targets were set and accounted for;
first bombers lifted off in a throb of engines
then thrusting missiles screamed and overtook them
all landing death at once -
no doubt there were surprises on the ground,
but don't listen to them -
it's just simple cries like a frog that's unlucky enough
to be overheard dying
from the natural conflict of things.

DebtLand

Owe, Canada!
our home-indebted land
true patriot slaves
your mortgages command!
with glowing loans we see rates rise
through fine print strong in fee
and stand outside what was our yard
when banks foreclose with glee!
God keep our banks
glorious with greed!
O finance industry we toiled for thee,
worked double shifts to meet your interest need.

Owe, Canada
our home-indebted land
true mortgage fear
in all wage-slaves command!
with pinching hearts we see suit guys
blow interest rates sky-high;
in sinking fear we ask ourselves,
if we sell, who will buy?
Bank, take these homes!
we cannot afford!
All our collateral goes overboard!
God save the bank which is our new land lord!
God, watch the bank which is our Brand New Lord!

Peter Revson

on the front page of the Friday evening Star
your face ink borders

your records
times you started from the pole
fastest laps
blur swift corners edging
you pass beyond the live word champions
in dusk news columns

black print spells
killed in practice
a photograph
taken your face in sunshine
smile hidden shadows

hand clashing gears
right foot forcing throttle thunder
seat thust harness
wind tight helmet roars the wall
blurs closer
wrist strain wheel twist savage
steel torn scream
grey sky turning plastic visor
your face empty

in the Friday Star
you face sunset silent
eyes cupped darkness
still image
Peter Revson racing driver
killed in practice

Dinner with Niki

That's Niki Lauda
at the second closest table sitting
just beyond Watson, the blonde grinning over
at you is James Hunt -
now he's facing this way,
staring back with the pale contemptuous eyes
of a World Champion twice come here for the Grand Prix only;
this is a man who hates fans asking
for autographs or how the pink skin feels
on his grafted forehead and once-blistered hands-
see the toothy grimace he makes at me
for even daring to wonder how it was
to be almost burned to death and make practice time
six weeks later in the backup Ferrari -
this man has guts and brains and drives the best
in the world perhaps -
bon appetit, cheri;
I can hardly eat for watching him.

Images: Gilles Villeneuve

From the clutter of my top dresser drawer
an old race program
folds open
        on a crumpled page
                your face
bright sun dark shadows
hand writing over it
        "best wishes"

Grand Prix weekend
July and humid at Watkins Glen on Friday
in the restaurant lobby after Dinner with Niki
waiting small and blonde and quiet by yourself
without the flashing red Ferrari
 - V twelve cylinders screaming -
no nomex did we catch you out of uniform
                standing
                      still
I notice you
        an autograph please
surprised to be asked unhappily recognized
   you bend at the counter preparing to sign my program
my French is rusty high school   you don't speak much English
Bill Newton
        so we have no conversation
                      watching
each other as you take my pen

You are being nice to a fan to me a stranger
but I know your every move
I have followed you with binoculars in the grand stand turn
a fast right hander
sliding across the pavement forcing the fastest line

Retirement Clock

accelerating
at the edge of control toward the paddock bleachers
the engine scream
                up shifting
even the infield campers and beer heads
pivot
they have heard of you coming
                            fast
cars, Swiss house, cute wife
brunette and petite the papers say afraid
of your black beliefs on the outcome of risks
so I goggle and beg you to wish yourself well
to get back to her

good luck
      and thanks
for your name on my program over the photograph
of your helmeted face
the ballpoint slipping
                black squiggles
                            like wheel skids
not quite losing control
                in your impatience
                            to begone
bright sun dark shadows

Looking down on your image I whisper from your future:
On Sunday, the race
                your teammate Scheckter
falls back because of tires
next week the whole new circuit at Montreal
is shouting your name
next year
your prophecies of danger racing death
                come true

NoteBook: Galapagos' Worlds

tourists
a foreign world
like blue-footed boobies
we waddle past their whistle-honk
talking

land legs
walk weird at sea
one hand for railings, one
for camera binoculars
and you

step out
 - a savage world -
hush, shoe-footed tourists
to hear the lava land emit
bird cries

skin dive
in deeper worlds
green turtles sudden fish
breathless over spiny urchins
surface

we love
this foreign world
tanned faces Spanish smiles
the Samba rolls, a bell tinkles
dinner

circle
Daphne Major
what beak? what finch? sheer cliffs -
is this the place? hear Darwin's ghost
chuckle

Retirement Clock

sea legs
walk ill on land
for days this motion haunts
every step we take awake and
dreaming

return
to our own world
airline tickets cab fare
unpack children souvenirs film
laundry

talk from
memory's world:
wave albatrosses pass
the Samba waits at anchor our
panga

pictures
don't touch sharp rocks
can't hear Spanish echoes
birds wheel past volcano cliffs sea
lions

brief notes
relive that world
climb here step there the trail
is marked and guided: you lead we
follow

Thank you,
guide Bolivar;
gracias, Samba crew
your yacht remembered rides a swell of
welcome

Hiroshima

Hiroshima is just one test:
We need to know which bomb blasts best.
The patriotic thing to do
Is, flatten Nagasaki too,
To prove these weapons of the West.

Near child at home, how safe, how blest
To rest warm on your mother's breast;
God's aid, our airmen, damn, for you,
Hiroshima!

Far child of war, or foreign guest,
Proud Japanese, who beat the chest,
Fly flags of orange in our blue
Here comes a great surprise for two
Burned cities: citizens, impressed?
Hiroshima?

Cinquain 87: Matti's Flowers
(For Dmitri Baranovski)

> Who weeps,
>   when rain mourning
> washes the park in grief?
> cut flowers wilt, for you, blooms dropped
>   with Tears.

From G Ross Lord Park

I can't get the muck off
its leaves stuck with weeds
these shoes where've you been
came up by the street went away by the creek
clean dark enough now
and still
it's so easy to kick once somebody's down
now you're asking to be pushed around
you should know better
when we all wore black with our faces covered
you should know better
now you're asking to be pushed around
it's so easy to kick once somebody's down
and still
clean dark enough now
came up by the street went away by the creek
these shoes where've you been
its leaves stuck with weeds
I can't get the muck off

Afterward: in the Cemetery above the Reservoir

Afterward,
will grief flow
downstream past the reservoir,
or must it hide in depths
beneath a pane of ice
on top of which words falter like torn shapes
of rustling gusted leaves
or winded swallows diving and swerving close
to the flat and moveless surface
which they may not stir or touch

Afterward,
does grief find deeper speech
in the pious silence of icons, staring
over funerary niches
of names and blossoms shockingly fresh cut
they keep stiff vigilance
but their saintly eyes
lead ours to look where their faces read inscriptions -
angelic mouths move for whispered benedictions
that are lost in the same cold wind
that plucks and scatters dry petals amid dead leaves
sent below us, hidden, to the reservoir
of sadness ebbing slowly onward
allowing an ice to frost across it

How deep must the grief go,
to be mute and frozen,
and what are the words that emerge from weeping,
Afterward?

The Message of Gary Gilmore

This is a holdup:
black pistol cocking at your face
till drawer jingles palmslick silver
masked sneers gun barrel poking
- let's do it

Bang gavel courtroom
electric chair gas chamber noose condemned
air conditioned lawyers argue life sentences
do you stand prisoner to challenge justice?
- let's do it

Pin bright the target
black shirt spot white to fix the heart of a man
hooded beyond five sighted rifles
five fingers squeeze out thunder shouting
- let's do it

The Silence of Gary Gilmore

Stand hooded dark
eyelashes scratch night blinking I hear
brass cartridges click rifles loading
black sleek barrels menace
my lawyers losers disappointed soon
it will be over, it will begin
to kill trapped strangers pacing death row cells
caught up in justice

Sit tight coarse tunic scratching wrists
tied arms itch hot
chill stethoscope come search my heart for death
a becoming target
be accurate be quick I flinch
bang muscles jerk white pain contracted chest
time stops child murder calling up red sandpiles
mother play castles spill shapeless down   my blood

Dream Meredith

how does your dream last morning?

chill grey concrete walls your bed
hunched pillow shadows
close toilet trickles haunting sleep
swirling tortured explanations
splash words jumbled rapid
night shapes beating ringing ears
shriek spiral currents choking
sucked under

steel bars cast net patterns cross your cheek
shut eyes twilight caught -
how many families dollars borrowed
hitch hike truckers long run sunsets
left hungry houses
clock tick midnight bulblit kitchens
waited creaking paint chipped chairs
late locking doors
how does your dream last morning

Retirement Clock

sixteen years of age and able
how do you plead not guilty
how do you turn back stranger faces
accusing eyes your honor
grey lawyer wrinkles courtroom murmurs
one question
how do you plead
how do you plead
how do you dream last morning

wake last morning
rough wool blanket tumbles bare your throat
thick swallow
smooth damp toes press stone
pale sheet prison naked grasped
tremble fingers linen strips cry tearing
cell dark muffles
knots jerk nightmare tight
how does your dream last morning

cloth hiss slither iron ceiling rods
step up this way the toilet chuckles
between cold feet
stained porcelain whirlpool whispers
- how do you plead -
black gavel falling pulsing neck words stopped
sixteen years of age and able
how does your dream plead guilty
last morning

Whipper Billy Watson

Your picture in the paper woke the ghost
of my father sitting close to television
grey ribbon images
twist wrestlers heave and tumble near the ropes
thump sweating close-up
the Black Avenger tugs your thinning hair
Dad mutters between clenched teeth and sips of beer
our lips snarl pain as knees compress
your shoulders touch the mat: One... Two...
- the ref is counting -
your face a mask of force in fierce control
one shoulder lifts neck muscles twitching
our throats call out together
- if the Whip gets up that bastard best look out -
quick champion we urge you
we clench our wills to make you break the hold
and stay our hero.

You fought for us
roar sweet acclaim of half a million fans
chanting your name you seemed invincible
as time moved slowly weakening us all
investing careful earnings living well
within your means you made retirement late
past fifty and a victor in your age.

Retirement Clock

Few men achieve great ease in idle days
retirement met my father full aware
yet baffled by the sense of time and purpose
gone empty
slow television opera afternoons
became his feeble last enjoyment
and found him sleep within his easy chair.

Yet you still move in grace of voices cheering
and know how wide acclaim can stir a man
sending himself beyond his narrow peers
the newspapers print echoing your speech
and photograph you carrying one child
to reach all crippled children with your care
you touch my conscience with your sense of need.

My father often read what I was reading
over my shoulder answering aloud
I hear my voice repeat your charity
but Dad retired too early
remembering you warrior of the canvas
old champion
your picture in the paper touched his ghost.

Evensong: What Time Has Left

What time has left my father creeps
to prowl his den dust record heaps
worn scratches play his coming night
waltz tempo dreams to old delight:
he holds my mother now he sleeps.

Grey office closing daylight seeps
though middle age my evening sweeps
wife dinner making love polite
what time has left.

Undressed for bed my small son weeps
for promised stories up he leaps
sit still my dwarf and I recite
the prince who came to wake snow white
kiss magic lovers no spell keeps
what time has left.

Helmeted

On our Internet News screen
you, sullen soldier, slouch, smoking,
hatless at twilight,
restless in camouflage heavy clothes.

Reaching with the **mouse** to -*switch images*-,
I see my face as you reflected,
as if I flick your cigarette and lean
to peer beyond the combat broken trees
that cower like refugees ahead of grey treading tanks
mounting crushed rubble that might have marked a street

what do we see?

look out in the marching darkness
are those muzzle flashes or sparks of snow?
is the final **click** guns? -*loading*- as
we put our helmets on.

A Work for Peanuts
(for Charles Schultz)

With drawn
 small characters
Schultz shared a gentle world
 sad magic, messenger retired,
withdrawn

 Good Grief
what news is this?
 you made us laugh alive.
your favourite oxymoron ends:
 good grief

The Satan Clause

He has horned friends.
He exploits smaller people.
He shows up entirely red except for white hair like fur.
He appears in hearthfires and seems to sneak down chimneys.
He bribes little children with presents.
He travels clandestinely at night across international borders.
He keeps a low profile when not distributing goods of dubious origin.
He has never been audited for taxes and has no visible source of income.
They say he has ways of getting up on the roof and then into your house.
He uses wild animals for transport.
He makes you wait for a year.
If you didn't get what you were promised, tough luck.
He has never been sued.
He keeps a list, and you're on it.

Earl Goes to Egypt

Too late now
as mummies are all wrapped up and gone
so you are too
entombed in tombs   engraved on gravestones
your life will never inspect theirs
or their deaths either

fortunately
when the "Treasures of Tutankhamen" came to town
you visited all their gold in a wheelchair
with a tape and a guide to explain you around sarcophagi
and stiff face masks
the witnesses of rich life centuries lost

now I pray for you
you were weak and silly sometimes, and a good man too
much missed
is it hot and dry there
would the devil or god assign you to Egypt
to haunt some pyramid for a century or two -
I think you'd like that,
become the official curse of Tutankhamen:

don't touch my artifacts don't do graffiti
on my sacred walls
   of death

From Bexhill Court

I wake up in the narrow kitchen
of our chilly apartment I am twenty-four
years old again and the plug-in toaster
still needs fixing on wobbly feet
I stand in the pinching gap between sink and table
and can reach any dish open every drawer
for that was what our marriage was like, then:
all the heat we needed came from our bodies
and we could touch each other everywhere -
but our spirits were bursting those walls at the seams
too full for such close accommodations
and so success and time
had us wake up older in wider rooms
grown up with family but no more need
to bump into each other
any more, lots of space
to let us lead these dreamed-of, richer lives.

What Happened to Campus Women?

slouching
too serious
faces closed over books
squint eyes don't flirt they don't wear skirts
no smiles

girls once
were beautiful
wise eyes subtle gestures
sweet sense of self, so generous
like love

Retirement Clock

nice fake oak
and antique Roman numbers
there's a panel at the back
you lift by a finger hole to see where the D cell goes
this time
needs no pendulum to swing back
it's a sealed quartz movement
showing hours, minutes, seconds, and phases of the moon -
a calculating gift for the end of a working life
tick tock close it up

here's the little plaque that goes with the clock
pure brass of course and mentions you by name
the gratitude of a laying-off company extends
throughout the echoing house
chimes on the quarter hour plays on the hour
choice of Dick Whittington gongs or Westminster bells
even those notes are synthesized today
tock tick

imagine what would happen if the clock ran backwards
untelling the story
of all that time
                spent at work of course
the anticulmination of a lifetime of effort
up to one naive graduate anxious for a job
remembering
to see the quarter century of promises
undone

Not Resolved

I watch my daughter cross to the waiting school
and remember, sixteen years old, walking away.

She was just this age and I was not much older
and certainly no wiser than Spring robins
that call across the traffic space between us;
our futures were less clear than horoscopes
in the rattle of newspaper pages
that blow like tumbleweeds in the curbside gutter
turning
themselves to old and tattered messengers.

I am sure she forgot me,
went ahead into her life like school corridors
whose branching choices
one officially could follow but won't feel welcome
to disturb
by visiting with personal questions.

It was not indifference
but powerlessness
to resolve what our wills and bodies thought they wanted
when our minds and selves were still not sure enough,
not willing as the robin to start commitment
with a single twig or a bit of twine;
not ready to settle down for common stories
when we still thought that our own exploits
could make headline lives every day, starting soon, tomorrow,
a respected startling feature
read out on our street of progress,
well-lit, smooth-travelled,
and comfortably busy.

Retirement Clock

So one goes off to school and I think about things.
Maybe I could have tried to get back in contact.
Doubtless the right decision was indecision,
no foolish presumptive action
no confession of love
and no request for the strength of reciprocation.

And it all worked out just fine as we both can see.
Obviously I've forgotten all about it,
flown on again as last year's robin,
and did as we then resolved
to get on with our headline, billboard-worthy lives.

For the Next Night Train

In the yellow dusk of the Simcoe station
we wait at the crossing black road steel tracks
for the next night train to come rumbling toward us
passersby speak soft questions to my Aunt
who whispers we are here only for this nephew
just what are we expecting,
they would like to ask
but she answers them first that it's a night time thing
can't get to sleep in a strange old bed
got to see one train come and count its cars like sheep
so they leave us waiting
for the next night train.

when the train does come it approaches with a grumble
it's quite dark now and I sort of wake up
from the station bench
we wander to the road again the white barriers dropping
stopping no traffic there's nobody here wants past
when the noise of steam hiss brings the locomotive
into the streetlights
chuff chuff pulses chug slowing for the station
one engine pulling
coal tender box car two flats three tankers
do you suppose a passenger could ride in that boxcar
or this caboose
lights passing slowly now rhythm rising rapidly
push push push push chant of the engine
fading
as the train goes accelerating off into darkness
and we start walking homeward
leaving the stationmaster waiting there alone
for the next night train.

Retirement Clock

Later I learned about railways and transport
how the little Simcoe town's folk met at the station
as the centre of newness, where shipments and people
came and later left, how the hub of social change
and fading hope
once slept or slouched there on worn wooden benches
marked "for ticketholders only"
who were waiting
for the next night train.

Five thousand nights between child and adulthood,
twenty thousand more between vigour and age:
yes I know what time it is.
Can you spare one evening for me, my young Nephew,
with such big changes coming rumbling ever closer
I might have the courage to go down to the station
if you could come with me as my anchor to the future
to hear "punch my ticket please" I will need to sit down
there will be casual questioners that noone really answers
just idle chatter you need not listen to
about rest in the darkness or late fellow travellers
among the few of us still left to spend our shrinking time
waiting
for the next night train.

Pirouette with a Rose in your Teeth

party rumours grow
swirling round Pierre Trudeau;
lost chapters fall
silent under drowning snow;

fresh flowers fade
how his lovely maid
given children three
exits to be someone free

true forces last
beyond a separatist blast
flapping flags still fly
bowed heads proud maple leaf on high

let frosted roses weep
frail crimson watchers of his keep
from time and age, should we dare call
how might he answer from such sleep?

In Halifax Citadel

Redcoats with drums come marching,
  changing the summer guard;
orders sharp as bayonets
  echo over the yard.

This living pattern of soldiers
  wheels at the steps of the past
as the redcoats climb their citadel
  to keep watch on an ocean vast.

Do not look too keenly at faces;
  do not stare down a student's disguise,
but focus beyond on the traces
  from the age that they improvise.

There are foreign ships skirting the harbour
  for the cannon mouths on these walls
and a hundred tunics and muskets
  that move when their captain calls.

There are farms to the south and to westward
  are new settlers clearing the trees;
there are buildings and children dependent
  on the citadel guarding the seas.

Do not peer too closely in faces;
  let the red coats march their spell
of clattering boots on stonework
  from the time that their echoes tell.

Orders quick as bayonets
  rattle across the yard;
redcoats, drums, and marching
  honour a ghostly guard.

Jim Bennett   Poems 5

To Crows Returning

Come melting snow call early crows, my summons;
spring perfume typists watch me leave my office
glass exit face the new west wing would shield me:
brick walls close off the forest of decisions
begun an ended innocence ago.

ambition moved me, back
to this building of narrow branching corridors
Head Office stayed and grew
still faces know me, older and astonished
some pause for names to stumble on our lips.

Outside rain afternoon flat whispers pavement
I choose my way between parked cars and puddles
wet shapes, new models, paces splat reflections:
no one ever comes back the same
I begin the frost-soft slope to the waiting wood.

Hard years have left me
more than gold-filled pens and written names
on thankyou cards at farewell business lunches:
opinions forced through difficult assignments
things done and undone end naive perceptions.

Fog hissing breath I enter dim grey trees
flakes blurred positions dreams melt way before me
defenceless steps ghost down the gaping hollow
where shadows gathered round the judgement thicket
call black crows, come back, ready, now they find me.

Old Tracks

snow over tracks
like rust on rails
reminds: we can not come so often
yet arrived before frost's grip relaxes
stiff soil crunched under tight ice boots
arthritically pacing
if your cane-punched holes cross steps of deer prints
where the rock cut marches
the old train way between stone into forest
then we are at large outdoors again
in an awkward eagerness too early for violets
not late enough for catkins
here the narrow curving path of forgotten boxcars
keeps shaded drifts from dazzling sunlight
looking up
your whiteness of hair glows haloed just as it was
on our first springtime coming together
today we touch awkwardly holding tight against cold
each other's mended mitten fingers
like rust on rails
while behind us certain as age time's wind is drifting
snow over our tracks

Relapse

somehow
I came back, hot
for your body, eager
over meals, conversation: where
was I?

Drab Ending

turning
twisting downwind
my coloured garden propellers spin their prism
OrangeYellowGreenBlueVioletRed
under leaf-gusting maples
sometimes reversing
RedVioletBlueGreenYellowOrange
before the central pivot also switches
returning
GreenBlueVioletRedOrangeYellow
It's autumn and a time of changeful air
soon these altered final leaves will also leave
blowing down earth-brown like death
for burial in seemly random patterns
but like my end of life seen through one window
as last blush cardinals
prepare departure plumages
my blurred reflection catches breath on glass
white-frosted, cold and fragile
overlooking grey dry leaves
in a tattered housecoat
trying to remember fading shades
GreenYellowOrangeRed
VioletBlueBrown
drab, dun
nothing

In Thorn Wood

The path through the wood walks right up to my farmhouse
skirting this new sun room like an add-on silo
of glass and concrete

There are rabbit tracks out there in the snow
and the pond at the end of the lawn is starting to thaw
but things move on so slowly, even though time speeds up

If I urge my arms they can reach the wheelrims
I can choose to sit in sun or sleep in shade
but my limbs go lax to let the last snow buntings
come down to me

Up there in the careless sky an invisible jet
carries hidden folk through unthinkable distances
from this far even a window wink is unlikely
I can see the contrails bend and move past the treetops
as if the clearing were urging them out of sight
so the innocent birds could come down where my outstretched
hand
would feed them, if I could just put on my coat
and go out to them

Retirement Clock

At the end of the path I know is a thorn bush frozen
with last night's rain gone solid in sudden cold
as the winter pounced once more like a thing determined
to live one more day one more season one more
lifetime of waiting for birds to deign to land

like me the thorn bush marks what was once lush pasture
now my meadows are full of rotten roots fit for burial
and silence broken by calls of birds and wind
hypnotically moving the evidence away
of my life turning to dreams and memories
like words said out of doors with the muffler tight
and the snow mitts white and easy lifting the latch
on the pasture gate

into the final vacancies
of the frozen pond
and an empty sky.

Baracoa: Max's World

I

as guide
you misled us
talked round Baracoa
as if your world's one novelty
were us

(Baracoa: Max's World)

II

We know Christopher Columbus
landed here, because
of his clear description: round harbour, almost
perfectly circular, square anvil mountain
looming up to the west, freshwater river and sandbar
but we think our cross is not from Spain
tests show it is native wood.

These amulets
called bull's eyes, are really
hand-sized tree seeds worn by waves
collected up gravel beaches
and necklaced on cords for tourists to buy
from insistently bargaining children.

No you're not allowed to make photos
of the museum's outside primitive statues.
inside we will be permitted
but the light is not strong.

On creaking bicycle rickshaws, elderly tourists
are taxied round town.
if you came to stay longer
you would find we have four fine hotels
we'll walk up this steep driveway to see one.
*Looking down on the town the view of pool and anvil
and circular harbour is perfect.
Too bad that rusting old hull in the foreground basin
hasn't been moved or sunk.*

*Like a step into some other time, Baracoa
is beautiful, artificially peaceful:
until a hundred years ago
they did not have an access road.
You just lived and died there.*

Have they told you the story of La Pelou?
before the road the inhabitants
were mostly Spanish, Indian, with a few French
families all interbreeding
and one day this most hairy man
appeared from nowhere possible
to wander about Baracoa,
which he did for six weeks.
no one cared to talk to him
nor asked him whence he came or why
but I'm sure our younger boys all teased him
and everyone that could crossed the street
so as not to be breathing downwind of him.
nobody knew if he ate or where he slept.
they didn't think he spoke any language
or understood at all
until that last day
when he strode to the centre of town and denounced
each and every one of us face to face
with all our descendents
to the end of time in perfect local Spanish
then walked away
and disappeared.
all around town then were forests.
there is even a picture.

Retirement Clock

we take tourist snapshots
reboard the bus reboard the helicopter
return noisily to Sol Rio del Mares
all-inclusive resort on white sand beach
near Santiago de Cuba.
  that night in dreams I realize
  what it was about La Pelou that bothered me
  but cannot recall it when wakened.

was he some celestial tourist
judging, like us, town things from an outside light
of far other experience
did he want them to try selling trinkets
or to ride in a rickshaw
when he got to the only hotel then
was he told it was full

or did he simply come and go
on a schedule he could not control
in the hurry of his own outlander transport
with somewhere more pleasant to get to next
like us

(Baracoa: Max's World)

III

dear guide
we misled you
walking Baracoa
outsiders let you think they care
then leave

Certificate for Tania

blank grey face
pouch cheeks muscle white
mouth slow toneless thanking

wine thick carpet
crushed casters swivel office
black desk paper buried

wide short hands
thick fingers nails cut
filling chest empty room

white gold lettered   left punched holes
plastic binder   dark brushed hair
clay striped suit   shoes laced black

canadian, cancer, society, grateful,

loving, memory, daughter, tania,

no words meet those eyes

This is It

This is it:
plant your snow shoes well don't shake the tree by grasping
on sleet-thick needles of red pine
stiff and sharp with scaly branches bent
by the deep white hiding
all but the mound itself that shows us walls
once ended here
now your snow shoes stop their crunch with one last step
mine settle while the insidious icy breeze
keeps on moving things
making up sounds for smothered rooms to whisper
stirring the nerveless twig ends into gestures
and sifting
swept particles of drift so gathered
over our tracks to mask our passage.

does it end like this
must footprints merely cease
in a shapeless clearing two tracks blur to none
will all our walks together come to nothing
below zero
without words
no purpose but cast shadows traceless limbs
no more dreams held than these snow buried chambers
walked over
alike by man and brute   and trees
whose patient roots keep feeding underground?

Retirement Clock

We adjust our scarves and mittens
too cold for gloves too awkward to hold hands
I continue breaking trail and glancing backward.
Where I lead, you follow
among the shades of creaking cedars
as the wind mounts up to wake their twisted trunks,
over the frozen marsh whose beavers sleep,
through maple woods toward the marked path, roads,
the car and its heat, transport to civil locations
where cruder questions go unanswered.

You come beside on the wider space and gesture
which way leads back, round to our starting place.
This is it, I say.

Goodbye

sleek black car shut
she steps back
gate locked behind wide highway
her husband drives
crisp fall maples whisper
she climbs the left rut
bent tracks worn
into grass

lean brambles clutching pierce her dress
short breath catches stab held still
her forced smile freezes
sun pulses scarlet leaves
sway grey hair
white haloes stop her eyes

no science watches
red glass thermometers
needles stainless drug charts
electric heartbeats

she did unplug the kitchen toaster
the stove was cold
when breakfast ended
they drove the forest lane together
steel gate click
black door closing words
she strains to hear

goodbye

Moon Dreamer

Once awakened
he will fear swimming
but in deepening dreams he sinks to be one with his porpoises
in a dark ocean sounding on porpoise ears
muffled clankings and moanings from anchored buoys
steer sleek companions through his night
whose fin-pressures find his diving path
as he calls to them
in the breathless porpoise language of urgent clicks
and orders
they glide close together in ordered blindness
up from the sea-safe shelf toward moondream breakers
they combine close trust and fear and press on exultant
as he leaps surfacing
in his throat a wrong voice struggles and cries
betrayal waking
amid tangled sheets and afraid of water

The Lost Camp

I pee in the lake, like a fish
swimming naked at sunset
up the beach old dishes scoured with sand
are left to air dry next the tent that sighs
in a breeze that smells of smoke and pinesap only
here you say we can throw one apple core away
under each great spreading pine
when we are alone as this
on miles of empty shore

    now each dishwasher empties into a septic
    and everyone uses an indoor toilet
    can't drink the lake water

still in magic nights asleep in the oldest bed
of the modern cabin
lost wilderness comes back to call me
as a visitor in dreams I swim alone
in the bay after red dusk turns to melon moonlight
I can pee in the lake like a fish again if I want to
and the sandy shore is clean for miles, few footprints;
if I walked up suddenly onto the empty beach
could I pretend that you just finished scouring
those old chipped dishes;
if I had a light could I see your tracks in the sand
move back to the truck to tie the canoe down tight
and then drive off to the past with my dream dissolving
into liquid water
where I want to stay
with the feel of the flow of cool lake swim waves swirling
as I breathe in surfacing
to the smell of pines with the faintest trace of campfire
dreaming and sighing
like an empty tent

www.ingramcontent.com/pod-product-compliance
Ingram Content Group UK Ltd.
Pitfield, Milton Keynes, MK11 3LW, UK
UKHW022212230426
12048UKWH00016BA/809